Mel Bay's

Left-Handed

Children's Guitar Method 1

by William Bay

1 2

Visit us on the Web at www.melbay.com — E-mail us at email@melbay.com

How to Select a Guitar

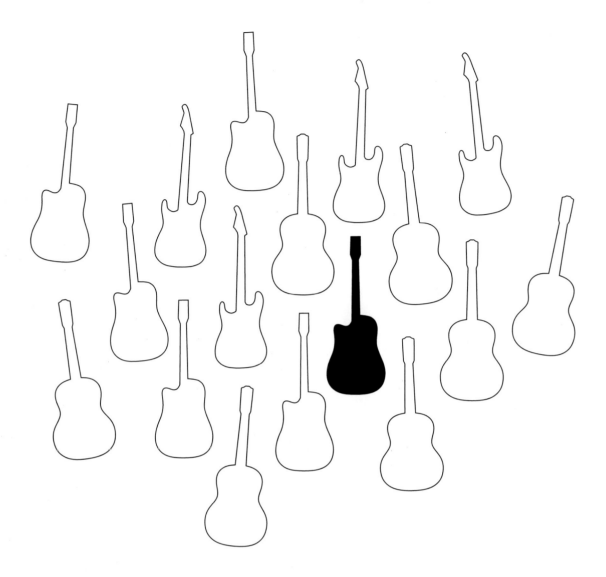

When selecting a guitar for a child, it is essential that the instrument obtained is not too big for the student. In many cases, nylon strings will be easier for the student to begin on; however, many students do begin successfully on steel strings. For most children, I recommend a student size or a three quarter size guitar. In addition, you must make certain that the neck is not too wide. This is especially important if you are going to start the student on a nylon string guitar. Many nylon string guitars have very wide necks. Your local music store can assist you in selecting the instrument. Be sure to take the student in and let the student hold the instrument to see if it is manageable. It is a good idea to check the strings to make certain that they are not too high off of the fingerboard at the nut, or first fret. (Consult the parts of the guitar diagram to see where this is.) Also, your teacher may help you check whether or not there are string buzzes on up the neck and whether or not the instrument plays in tune on up to about the 7th and 8th position. Most of the student model guitars being made today are of a very good quality and many of the problems which used to plague beginning guitarists are no longer concerns.

NOW AVAILABLE...A 60-minute video is now available which contains all the teaching content contained in this book. This video is highly recommended as a valuable learning aid and supplement to this guitar method. Also available are a split-track, play-along stereo cassette, and a compact disc.

The Guitar and its Parts

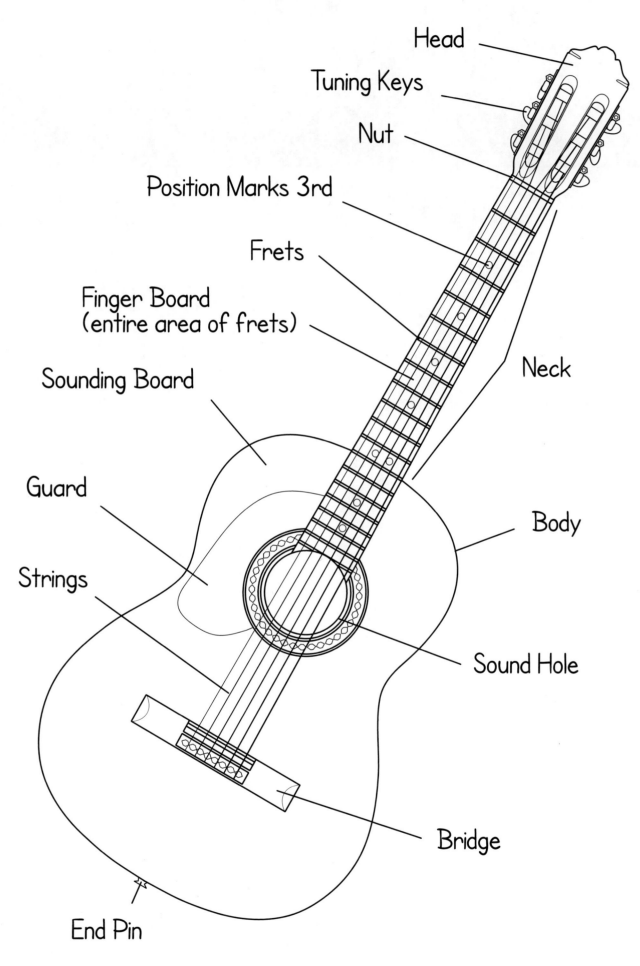

Head

Tuning Keys

Nut

Position Marks 3rd

Frets

Finger Board
(entire area of frets)

Sounding Board

Guard

Strings

Neck

Body

Sound Hole

Bridge

End Pin

How to Hold the Guitar

Fig. 1

Fig. 2

Fig. 3

Fig. 4

Fig. 5

First, grab hold of the guitar as shown in fig. 1. Next, bring it in close to the body as shown in fig. 2. Next, bring the left hand to the position shown in fig. 3. This is to bring the guitar firmly up against your body. The right hand is then moved, as shown in fig. 4, up into the area of the first position. This is where the first finger is resting in the middle of the first fret. Finally, fig. 5 shows the left hand getting ready to strum the strings of the guitar.

Strumming the Strings

Fig. 6

Fig. 7

At this point in the student's learning process we will be concentrating on coordinating chord fingering in the right hand with strumming motion in the left hand. We, therefore, recommend strumming with the thumb down across the strings. Later on we will introduce the possible use of a pick.

To strum the instrument, place the thumb by the sixth string. This is the largest of the six strings (figure #6). To strum down across the strings, bring the thumb down gently across all six strings. Do this a number of times until all of the strings sound at once. The strum should be even and the thumb should not rest too long on any one string. You should glide evenly across all six strings (figure #7).

The right hand should be positioned on the neck of the guitar so that the thumb rests comfortably in the middle of the back of the neck. This will require you to arch your hand somewhat. Look at the photos on page 5. By keeping the right-hand thumb in the middle of the neck, and by learning to play in this fashion from the beginning, your fingers will have the tendency to come down directly on top of the strings and avoid the problems of accidentally lying across the wrong strings when you finger notes and chords.

RIGHT HAND POSITION

When you lay your fingers across the wrong strings, you will accidentally deaden the sound of some of the notes. Proper positioning of the right hand will give you great freedom in fingering rapid passages later on. Also, by placing the thumb in the middle of the neck, you are providing maximum strength in fingering difficult chords.

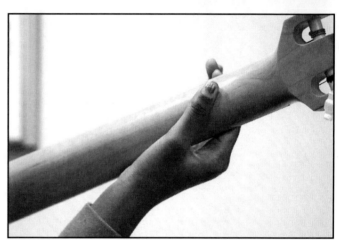

THE RIGHT HAND

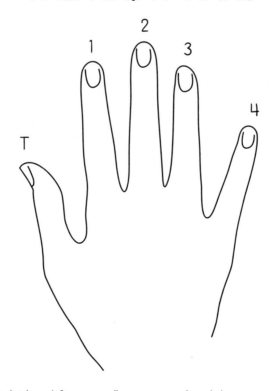

Numbers for the right hand fingers will appear in chord diagrams throughout the book.

TWO WAYS TO TUNE THE GUITAR

1. The six open strings of the guitar will be of the same pitch as the six notes shown in the illustration of the piano keyboard. Note that five of the strings are below the middle C of the piano keyboard.

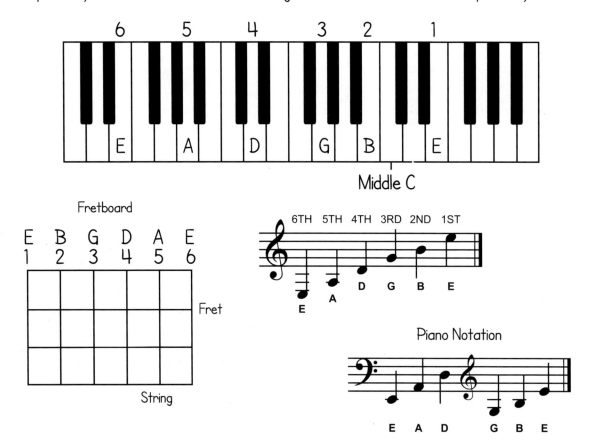

2.

1. Tune the 6th string in unison to the E or twelfth white key to the LEFT of MIDDLE C on the piano.

2. Place the finger behind the fifth fret of the 6th string. This will give you the tone or pitch of the 5th string. (A)

3. Place finger behind the fifth fret of the 5th string to get the pitch of the 4th string. (D)

4. Repeat same procedure to obtain the pitch of the 3rd string. (G)

5. Place finger behind the FOURTH FRET of the 3rd string to get the pitch of the 2nd string. (B)

6. Place finger behind the fifth fret of the 2nd string to get the pitch of the 1st string. (E)

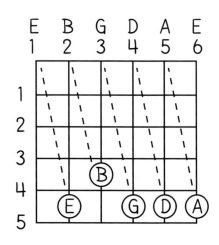

PITCH PIPES

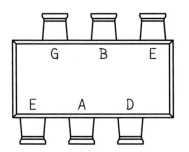

Pitch pipes with instructions for their usage may be obtained at any music store. Each pipe will have the correct pitch of each guitar string and are recommended to be used when a piano is not available.

For more instruction on learning to tune your guitar—
see *EZ Way to Tune Guitars*

G CHORD – EZ FORM

X = Do Not Play   O = Play

- Do not play the 6th and 5th strings
- 4th, 3rd, & 2nd strings are played open

Press the 3rd finger down on — ③ the 3rd fret on the 1st string

Open Strings

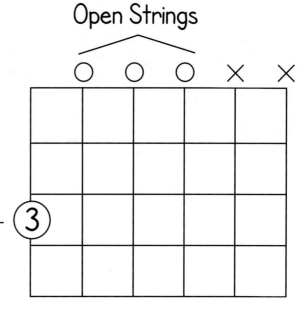

STRUMMING THE G CHORD

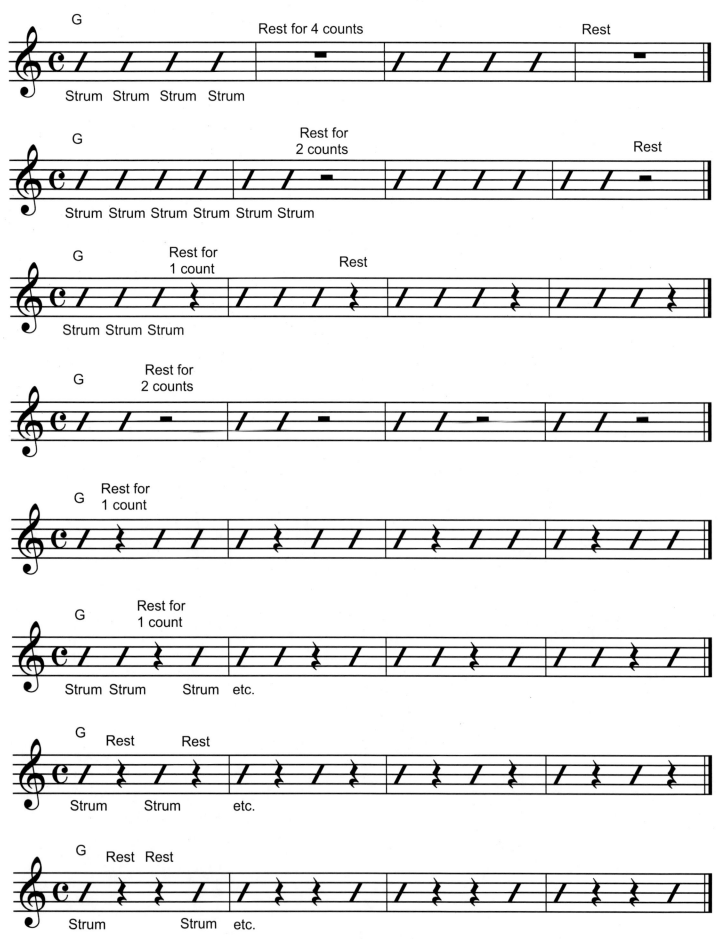

8

BROTHER JOHN – SING AND PLAY

9

C CHORD – EZ FORM

C Chord

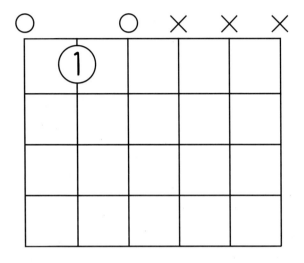

Play only
the top 3 strings!

Be sure your 1st finger does not
accidentally rest against the 1st string!

THREE BLIND MICE – SING AND PLAY

C

THREE BLIND MICE, THREE BLIND MICE, SEE HOW THEY RUN, SEE HOW THEY RUN, THEY

ALL RUN AF-TER THE FARM-ER'S WIFE WHO CUT OFF THEIR TAIL WITH A CARV-ING KNIFE, DID

E-VER YOU SEE SUCH A SIGHT IN YOUR LIFE AS THREE BLIND MICE. THREE BLIND MICE.

ROW, ROW, ROW YOUR BOAT

[Sing and Play]

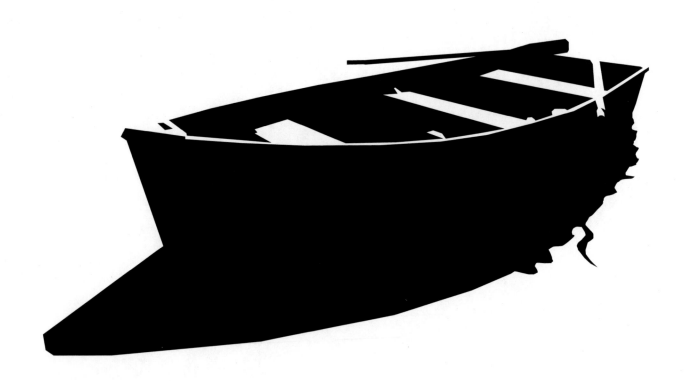

G7 Chord

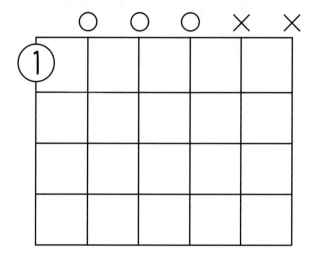

Play only the
top 4 strings!

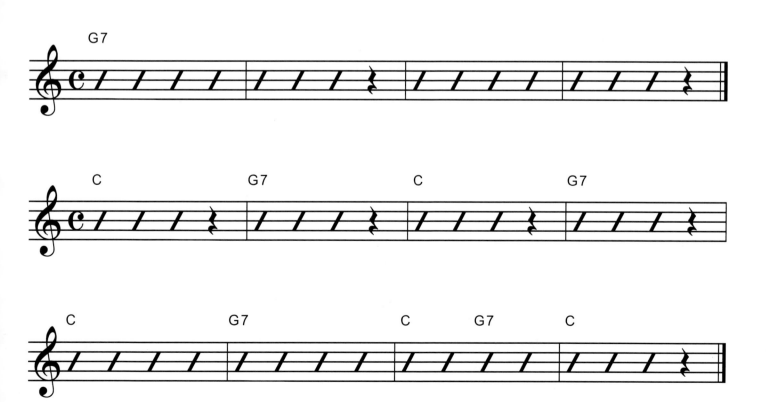

SKIP TO MY LOU

C
Left and Right   oh skip to my Lou
C
Left and Right   oh skip to my Lou
G7
Left and Right   oh skip to my Lou
G7   C
Skip to my Lou my darling.

LONDON BRIDGE

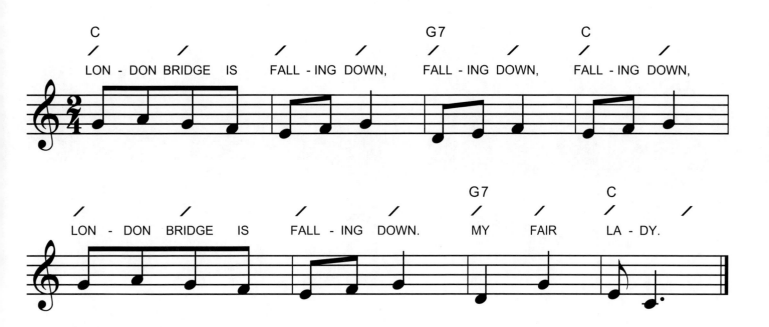

C CHORD – ADD FOURTH STRING

C

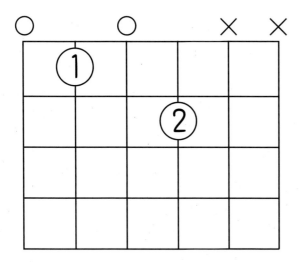

THIS OLD MAN

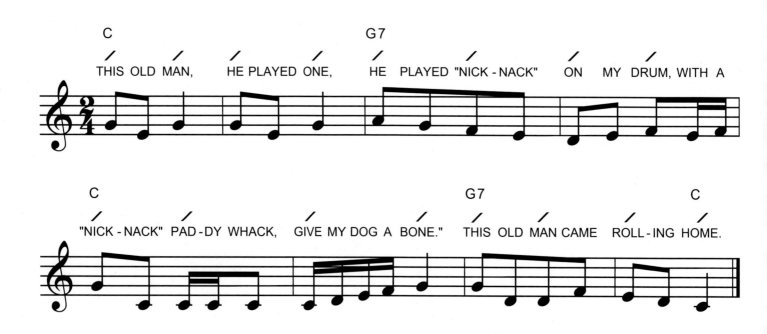

C THIS OLD MAN, HE PLAYED ONE, **G7** HE PLAYED "NICK-NACK" ON MY DRUM, WITH A

C "NICK-NACK" PAD-DY WHACK, GIVE MY DOG A BONE." **G7** THIS OLD MAN CAME **C** ROLL-ING HOME.

3/4 TIME

Up till now, we have played either 4 strums per measure (4/4 o **C**) or 2 strums per measure (2/4).

Now we will play 3 strums per measure (3/4).

COWBOY'S SONG

Count 1 – 2 – 3, 1 – 2 – 3, etc.

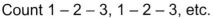

| C | G7 | C | G7 |
AS I_____WALKED OUT IN THE STREETS OF LA - RE - DO, AS

| C | G7 | C | G7 | C | G7 |
I WALKED OUT IN LA - RE - DO ONE DAY, I SPIED A YOUNG COW-BOY A

| C | G7 | C | G7 | C | G7 | C |
RID - IN' A PON - Y, O RID - IN' A PON - Y TO TOWN ON THAT DAY.

POP GOES THE WEASEL

Watch out for the rests!

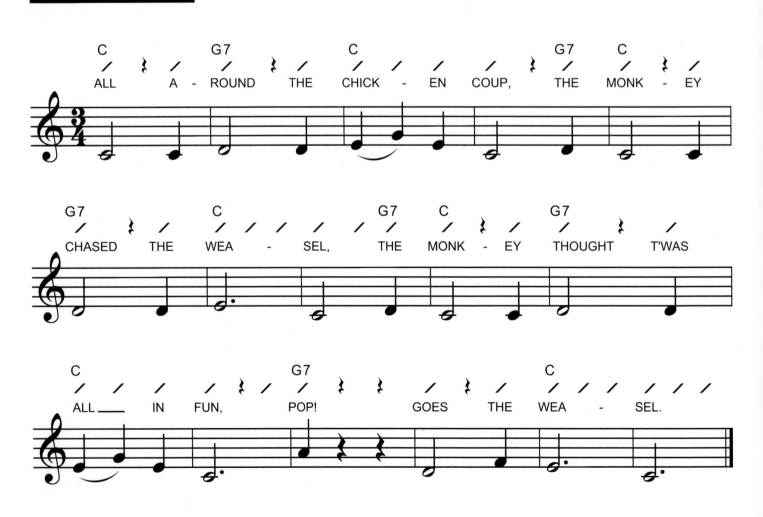

DOWN – UP STRUM

Up till now, we have only been strumming Down across the strings.
Now we will strum Down and Up.

/ = Down Strum   V = Up Strum

HE'S GOT THE WHOLE WORLD

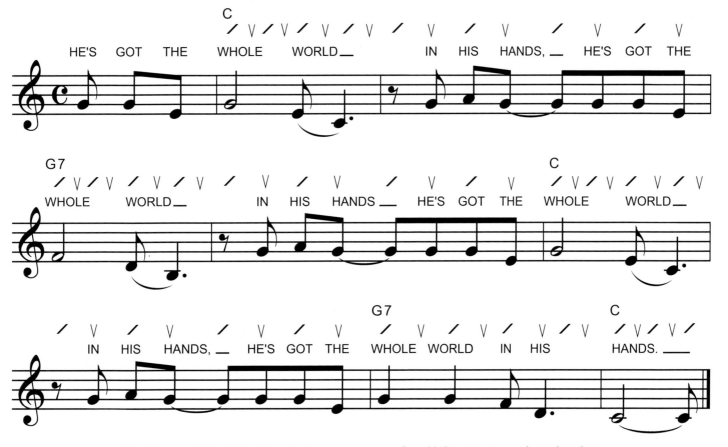

2. He's got the little bitsy baby....   3. He's got you and me brother....

BUFFALO GALS

THE FULL C CHORD

C

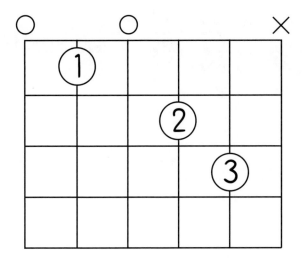

Play only the
top 5 strings!

Try now to play the full C chord. Practice it until the notes all sound clear, being certain that your fingers are not accidentally touching the wrong strings.

TRY TO USE THE FULL C CHORD

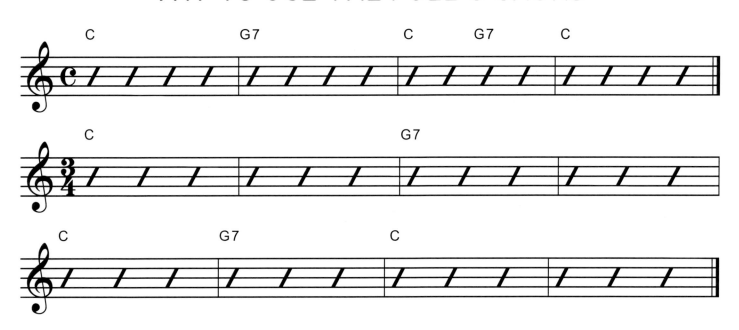

NEW STRUM

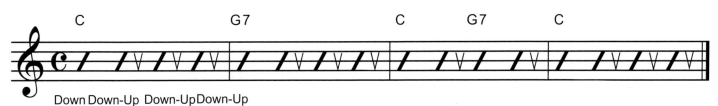

Down Down-Up Down-UpDown-Up

POLLY WOLLY DOODLE

OH I WENT DOWN SOUTH FOR TO SEE MY SAL, SING-ING POL-LY WOL-LY DOO-DLE ALL THE DAY MY SAL SHE IS A PRET-TY GAL, SING-ING POL-LY WOL-LY DOO-DLE ALL THE DAY. FARE THEE WELL, FARE THEE WELL, FARE THEE WELL MY FAIR-Y FEY, FOR I'M GOIN' TO LOU-SI-AN-A FOR TO SEE MY SU-SI-AN-NA, SING-ING POL-LY WOL-LY DOO-DLE ALL THE DAY.

HOLDING THE PICK

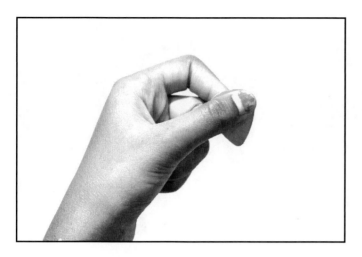

Now is the time to introduce the use of the flat pick. Study the photograph carefully, make certain that the pick is not held too tightly. Practice strumming up and down with the flat pick in order to get the feel of it. (The student may continue to use his thumb at this point if so desired by the teacher.) Make careful note of the symbols used to denote down pick and up pick. This will be used throughout as we learn to pick notes.

Check your hand position. Do not hold the pick too tight!

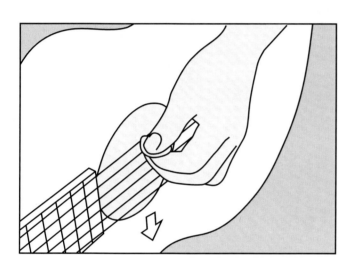

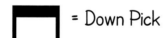 = Down Pick

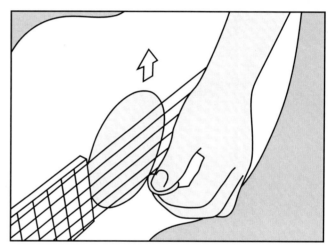

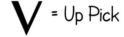 = Up Pick

A WORD ABOUT PICKING

The following note-reading studies begin with alternate picking. It is the author's belief that left-hand technique can best be developed by introducing the student to alternate picking from the beginning. This enables the student to gradually increase the tempos on practice studies without having to change picking technique to alternate picking at a later date. All studies should begin at a slow tempo. By now the student should have some feeling for the down-up motion of the hand as a result of the chord strumming previously done. You will notice that all of the beginning studies utilizing note reading and alternate picking require little or no string changes. The beginning studies do not even require fingering. Once the basic feeling for alternate picking is established, the student's confidence and flexibility will progress rapidly and technique will be fluid.

The teacher may at this point, however, choose at his or her own discretion to begin the note-reading studies with all down picking strokes. If this is the teacher's choice, then the author recommends the commencement of alternate picking on page 25 when eighth notes are introduced.

LEARNING ABOUT NOTES

Our first note is

E (MI)

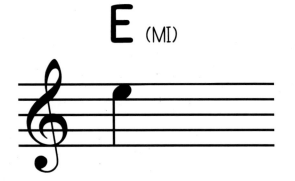

The 1st string on the guitar is called the high E string. Our first note is E on the open 1st string.

1st string open

E is first string open

PLAYING E

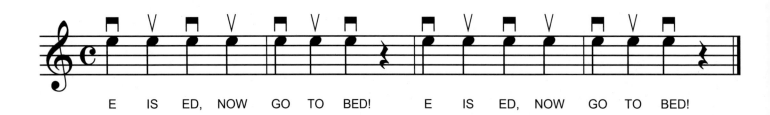

E   IS   ED,   NOW   GO   TO   BED!   E   IS   ED,   NOW   GO   TO   BED!

REST SONG

E in 3/4

COUNTING SONG

On the following song, we will play a new type of note called an Eighth Note. It looks like this (♪) or this (♫) or this (♬) Eighth notes get only half the time a quarter note ♩ gets. SAY the following song and play it.

I LOVE EATING DONUTS

Say and Play

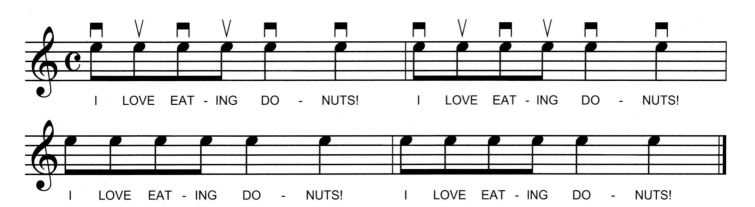

I LOVE EAT - ING DO - NUTS! I LOVE EAT - ING DO - NUTS!

I LOVE EAT - ING DO - NUTS! I LOVE EAT - ING DO - NUTS!

DON`T STEP ON ALLIGATORS

Say and Play

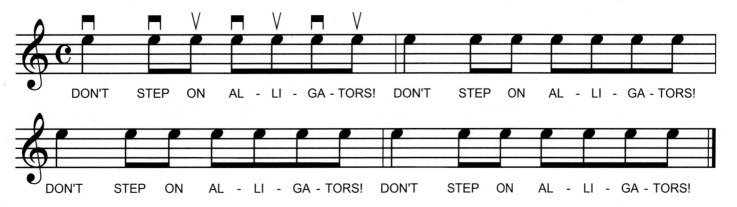

DON'T STEP ON AL - LI - GA - TORS! DON'T STEP ON AL - LI - GA - TORS!

DON'T STEP ON AL - LI - GA - TORS! DON'T STEP ON AL - LI - GA - TORS!

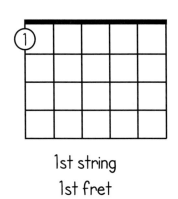

1st string
1st fret

F

F is 1st finger - 1st fret on the E string.

F IS FRED NOW SCRATCH YOUR HEAD

F IS FRED NOW SCRATCH YOUR HEAD.   F IS FRED NOW SCRATCH YOUR HEAD.

EATING COOKIES MAKES ME HAPPY

Say and Play

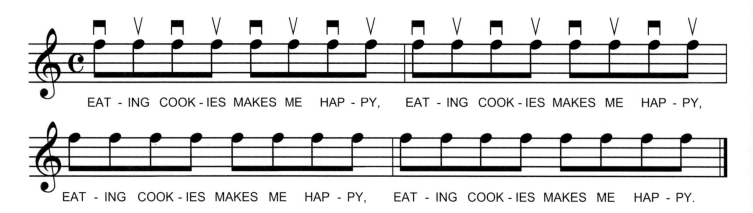

EAT - ING COOK - IES MAKES ME HAP - PY,   EAT - ING COOK - IES MAKES ME HAP - PY,

EAT - ING COOK - IES MAKES ME HAP - PY,   EAT - ING COOK - IES MAKES ME HAP - PY.

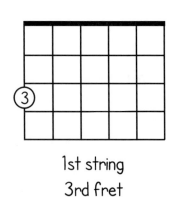

1st string
3rd fret

G

G is 3rd fret - 3rd finger

26

G IS GAIL GO PET A WHALE

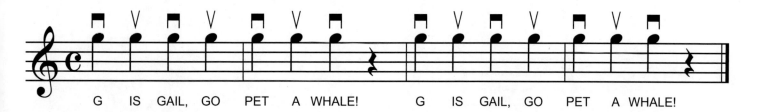

WON'T YOU CLIMB THE STAIRS WITH ME

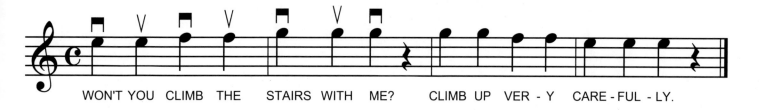

CHASING RABBITS

UP WE GO IN MY BALLOON

SEE SAW

B

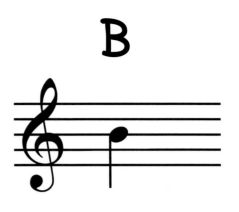

The 2nd string open is B

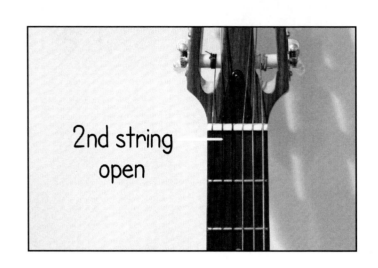

2nd string open

B is the 2nd string

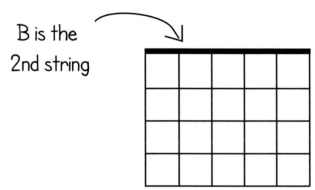

B IS BENJI

BEN - JI IS THE SEC - OND STRING, HE REAL - LY LIKES TO PLAY AND SING.

BENJI IS EATING CANDY

BEN-JI'S EAT-ING CAN-DY   HE JUST THINKS THAT'S DAN-DY.   BEN-JI'S EAT-ING CAN-DY   HE JUST THINKS THAT'S DAN-DY.

BEE BUZZ

BEE E BEE-E BUZZ-BUZZ   BEE E BEE-E BUZZ-BUZZ   BEE E BEE-E BUZZ-BUZZ   BEE E BEE E BUZZ BUZZ

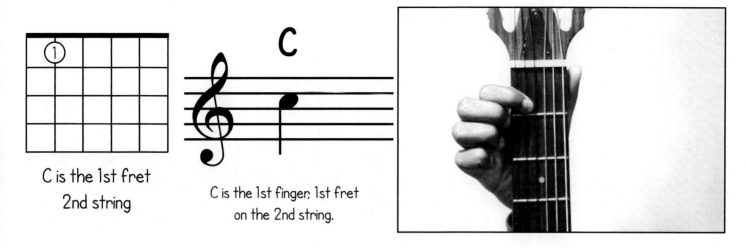

C is the 1st fret
2nd string

C is the 1st finger, 1st fret
on the 2nd string.

"C" IS CHRIS

C IS CHRIS, WELL LOOK AT THIS! C IS CHRIS, WELL LOOK AT THIS!

BEE SEE C B

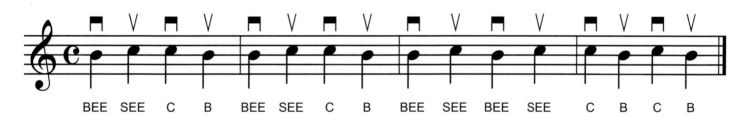

BEE SEE C B BEE SEE C B BEE SEE BEE SEE C B C B

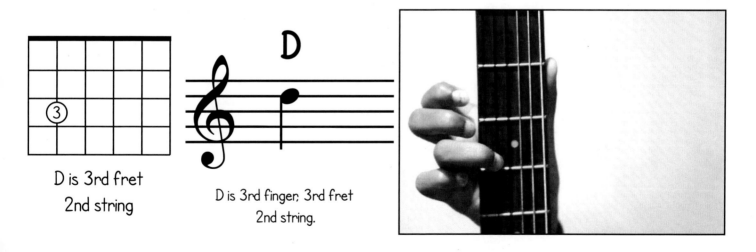

D is 3rd fret
2nd string

D is 3rd finger, 3rd fret
2nd string.

D IS DICK NOW FLICK THAT PICK! D IS DICK NOW FLICK THAT PICK!

PLAYING NOTES ON THE 2nd STRING

HAPPY SOUNDS

UP AND DOWN

SKIPPING

RUNNING

MARCHING

E AND B STRING

CLIMBING

SURPRISE SONG

INDIAN DRUM

SAILING

WALKING OVER HILLS

TURKEY WALTZ

D7

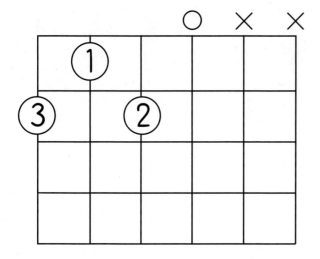

Do not play the bottom strings!

PLAY ONLY THE TOP 4 STRINGS

Play slowly and make certain each note in the D7 chord sounds clear.
Watch out for fingers accidentally resting on other strings and deadening the sound!

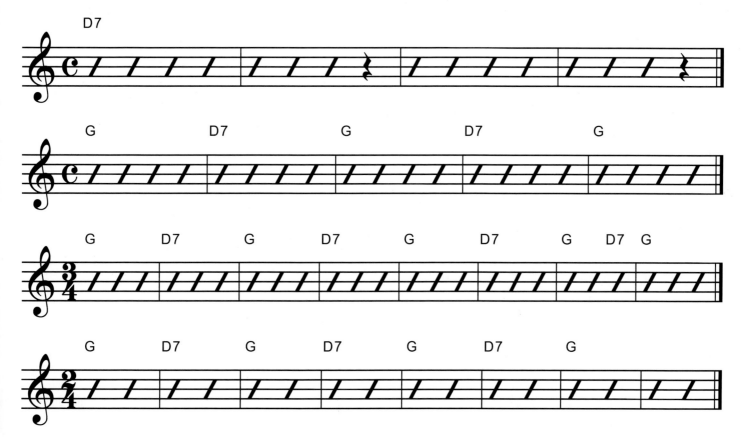

DOWN IN THE VALLEY

Sing and Play

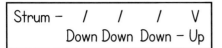

34

OH, MY DARLING CLEMENTINE

Sing and Play

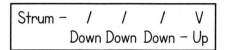

GO TELL IT ON THE MOUNTAIN

Sing and Play

YANKEE DOODLE

Sing and Play

LOOK OUT FOR THE C CHORD!

HOME ON THE RANGE

Sing and Play

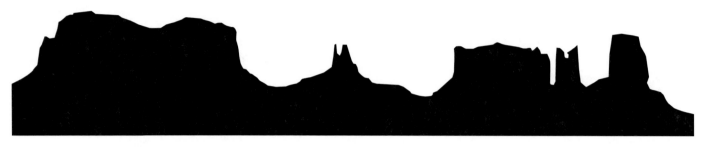

PRAISE HIM IN THE MORNING

Sing and Play

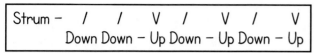

Strum – / / V / V / V
Down Down – Up Down – Up Down – Up

LOOK OUT FOR G7 CHORDS!

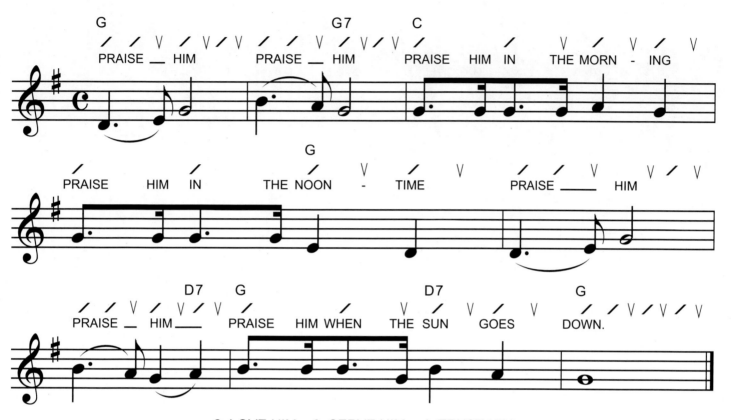

2. LOVE HIM   3. SERVE HIM   4. TRUST HIM

BINGO

Strum – / / / V /
Down Down Down – Up Down

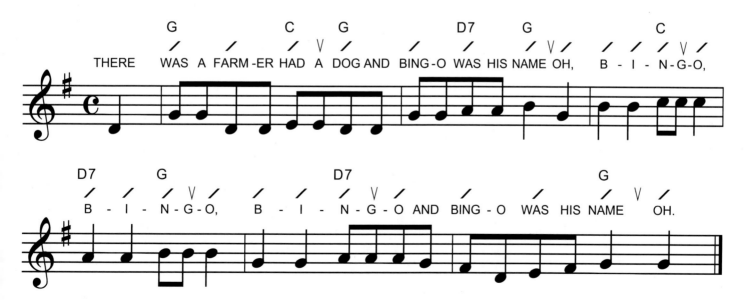

AMAZING GRACE

Sing and Play

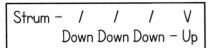

PEACE LIKE A RIVER
Sing and Play

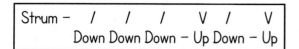

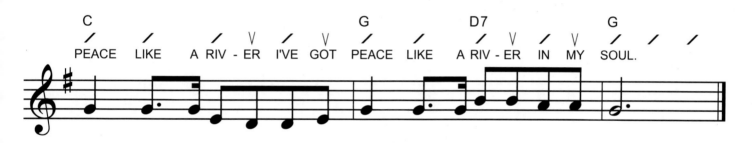

DO LORD

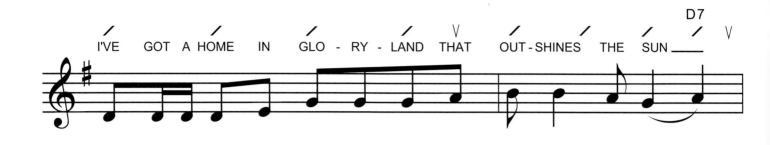

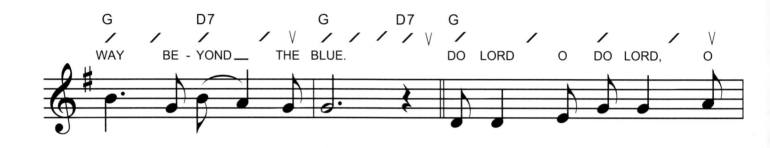

G is 3rd string open

G

The third string is called the G string.

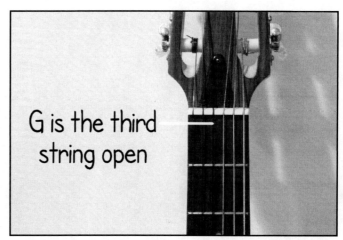

G is the third string open

G IS GA - RY HE'S SO SCAR - Y! G IS GA - RY HE'S SO SCAR - Y!

A

A is 2nd finger 2nd fret on the 3rd string

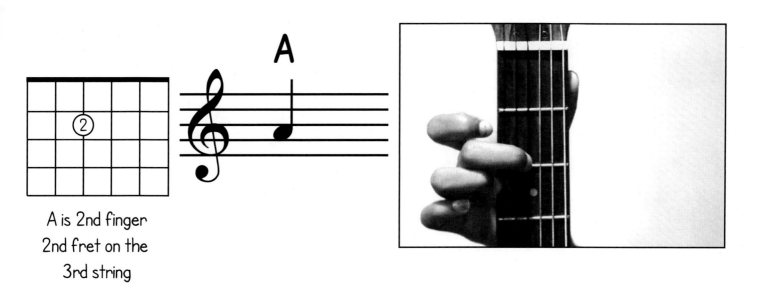

A IS ACE LET'S SEE HIS PLACE! A IS ACE LET'S SEE HIS PLACE!

GARY AND ACE

STUDY

HALF NOTE

This is a Half Note (𝅗𝅥)
It receives 2 counts

AU CLAIR DE LA LUNE

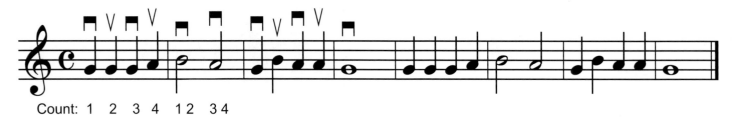

Count: 1 2 3 4 1 2 3 4

TWINKLE LITTLE STAR

JINGLE BELLS

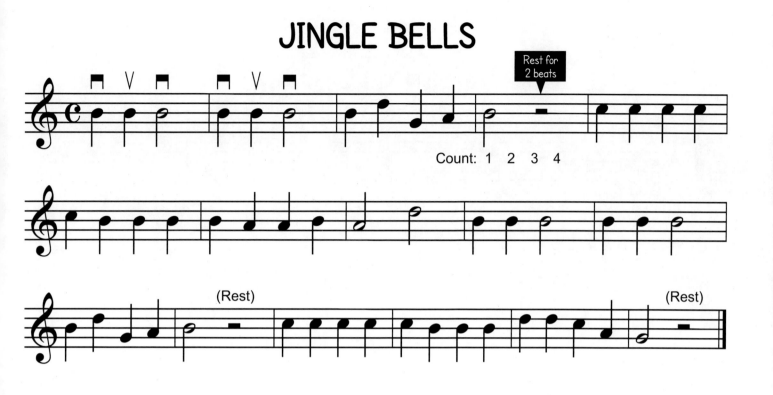

Count: 1 2 3 4

THERE'S A HOLE IN THE BUCKET

YANKEE DOODLE SOLO

DOTTED HALF NOTE

(♩.) gets 3 counts.
1 2 3

JACOB'S LADDER

Dotted half note

Count: 1 2 3 1 2 3

SURPRISE SONG

SPACE WALK

THE TIE

A tie looks like this (♩⌣♩) It connects 2 or more notes.
When you see a tie, pick the 1st note only.

RED RIVER VALLEY

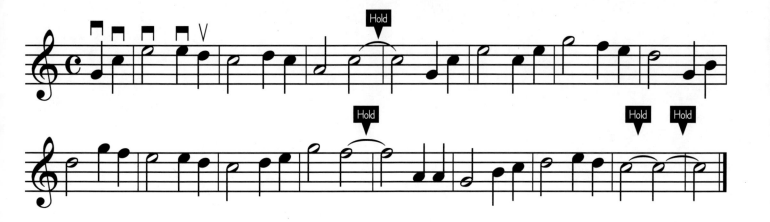

WHOLE NOTE

A whole note looks like this (o) It gets 4 counts.

O WHEN THE SAINTS

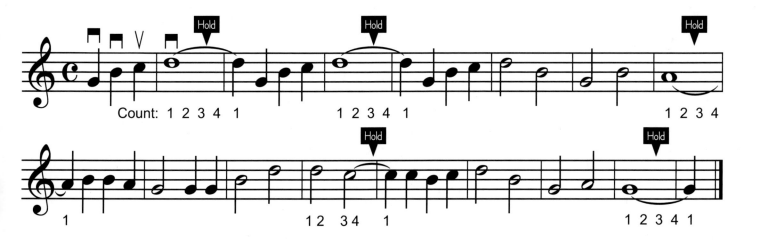

47